Kittens & Cats in color

by Angela Sayer

with an introduction by Christine Metcalf

Hamlyn
London · New York · Sydney · Toronto

Published by The Hamlyn Publishing Group Limited
London · New York · Sydney · Toronto
Astronaut House, Feltham, Middlesex, England
Copyright © The Hamlyn Publishing Group Limited 1971
Reprinted 1972
Revised edition 1975

ISBN 0 600 35333 8

Printed in Hong Kong by Dai Nippon Printing Company Limited

Kittens & Cats
in color

The noble Abyssinian of today closely resembles the sacred cat of the Ancient Egyptians, and is believed to be directly descended from a female brought to Britain from Abyssinia in 1869.

Introduction

If an opinion poll were to be taken on the popularity of various animals as pets, cats would come very high on a rating list. What is it that makes them one of the best loved of all domestic pets? They are appealing and aloof, independent and affectionate, they have dignity and elegance, in fact, they are a veritable Pandora's box of moods and characteristic traits. You never really possess a cat, more often it dictates its own terms but it will not abuse your generosity.

In terms of friendship the cat has much to give. There are many stories of cats who have undergone great privation and who have journeyed hundreds of miles in order to be reunited with loved ones from whom they have become separated. It is said that cats attach themselves to places, not to people, but this is untrue for cats are very loving although they have their own way of demonstrating their affection. Whether your pet is a tatty-eared alley cat carrying the scars of battle, or whether it is one of the many elegant pedigree breeds, if it has a mind to it will show the same devotion. It is said that in the fifteenth century Sir Henry Wyatt was flung into prison by Richard III for his loyalty to the Lancastrian party. A cat found her way into his cell and a friendship grew between the two. The story goes on to tell that this man's distress was great from starvation and cold but the cat was such a loyal friend that she visited every day and whenever she was able she would take him a pigeon. Her affection was obviously for the man for the cat is a comfort-loving creature and the cell must have been anything but inviting.

Variety is the very essence of the cat's make-up. One moment it can be lying before the fire, a coiled nebulous heap of fur, the next moment, with a yawn and a stretch, it has become as lithe and graceful as a ballerina. One moment you are housing a tiger in your hearth, then in an instant there is a gentle creature purring round your feet and craving your attention. Is it any wonder that for many years the cat was an object of worship? The ancient Egyptians identified the delicate lines of a cat with those of a woman, and they built a shrine to the cat-headed goddess, Bast, on an island completely surrounded by water. Many tomb paintings, frescoes and carvings are evidence of the esteem in which cats were held in the days of the Pharaohs. Mummified cats have been found in Egypt, some of them in mummy cases of great value. Herodotus, the Greek historian, wrote much about the value of cats in Egypt in ancient times. He relates that the penalty for killing a cat was death and that a Roman soldier was once practically lynched by an enraged Egyptian mob for accidentally killing a cat. If a dwelling caught fire the cat would be saved before any attempt was made to put out the fire, and, by law, when a household cat died, the entire family were required to shave their eyebrows as a sign of mourning. The honoured position held by cats in that society has never been equalled by any other animal. In northern Europe, too, the cat appeared in a religious setting. It was said the goddess of love and beauty, Freya, rode in a chariot drawn by two cats and that the trio represented fruitful love. Japanese geishas once subscribed for a funeral service for the souls of cats whose lives had been ended to provide catgut for the strings of the instruments they played.

In complete contrast to the adoration afforded to these creatures in ancient times, the Middle Ages was a bad time for cats. Pope Innocent VIII, in the fifteenth century, saw 'cat-worship' as a link with the Devil. The Inquisition legalized witch hunting and ownership of a cat was sufficient to invite arrest for sorcery. Many people, on slim evidence, were tortured and burned and their cats met a similar fate. The identification of cats with witchcraft continued until the eighteenth century—they were seen as the familiars of witches. There are remarkable stories of witches themselves taking cat shape. Cats are still seen as symbols of good or of bad luck—they are believed by some to indicate death and disease, to herald high wind or fine weather, to bring about happy marriage and the safe return of fishermen. All kinds of portents and omens are associated with cats. No other animal seems quite so versatile.

There is something especially appealing about all baby creatures. Psychologists believe it is the roundness of extreme youth and its wide-eyed innocence that casts a spell. Kittens are particularly attractive. Not only are they round and softly pretty but their playfulness and winning ways make them very hard to resist. Groups of kittens are a favourite subject for photographers, and a rewarding one, for what can be more charming than a group of kittens at play? Whether they are black, white, tabby, ginger or any other colour, they are all equally difficult to ignore, a bundle of enchantment to soften the hardest heart. Take a kitten into your home and you are assured of hours of entertainment, a certain rival to your television set, for you will watch it and play with it, cuddle it and tease it, until you begin to wonder who is really in charge, for if you let your attention wander to other matters your kitten will come to you and demand a game. And can you refuse those winning ways? Tiny, delicate paws soft as a whisper will come tapping your newspaper or tangling your knitting, encouraging you to throw a screw of paper, or begging you to trail a piece of string. Large wide eyes follow your every move, the kitten leaping and pouncing like the true hunter it is born to be. In his delightful poem about the antics of a kitten called *The Kitten and Falling Leaves*, William Wordsworth has drawn this very apt pen portrait:

'*. . . But the kitten, how she starts
Crouches, stretches, paws and darts:
First at one, and then its fellow,
Just as light and just as yellow;
There are many now—now one—
Now they stop and there are none:
What intenseness of desire
In her upward eye of fire!
With a tiger—leap half way
Now she meets the coming prey,
Lets it go as fast, and then
Has it in her power again:
Now she works with three or four,
Like an Indian conjuror;
Quick as he in feats of art,
Far beyond the joy of heart.
Were her antics played in the eye*

*Of a thousand standers-by,
Clapping hands with shout and stare,
What would little Tabby care
For the plaudits of the crowd?
Over happy to be proud,
Over wealthy in the treasure
Of her own exceeding pleasure.*'

A kitten is like all babies in that a game uses so much energy that suddenly it drops in its tracks, curls up and falls fast asleep in a fluffy ball of vibrating fur, preferably on someone's comfortable lap. Your kitten needs all the love and attention you can give it for it will be missing its brothers and sisters. All baby animals delight in playing in groups, tumbling and fighting with their peers. To find itself one day away from its mother and the rest of the litter must be a traumatic experience for a young kitten.

Let your imagination conjure a quiet room with a cosy fire. The mind automatically completes the picture by placing a curled-up cat delighting in the luxury of the peace and warmth. What more relaxing sight can there be than this? All cats love warmth and almost all the members of the cat family, including the big cats, the lions and tigers, live in warmer climes. No region is too hot for certain species. It is true that the snow leopard with its warm, furry coat, is found on the snowy mountains in Tibet and lynxes are found in Canada and Scandinavia, but these are exceptions; no cats of any description are to be found in the extreme north with the polar bear. It is thought that the cat's love of comfort first brought man and cat together to begin what has become a lasting association. Camp fires of the early cavemen probably drew the cat from the darkness and cold outside to share the cheerful blaze. The men would have thrown odd scraps of meat to their four-legged visitors and in return the cat would have reduced the number of rodent scavengers. Thus began a very satisfactory relationship which has continued from time immemorial up until the present day.

A yawn exposing a rough pink tongue and fangs,

This trio of Red Tabby kittens, ready to go to their new homes, are in glowing health as may be seen by their clean appearance and shining eyes.

bright and fine as a needle, are a reminder of your pet's fierce ancestry. It does not require too much imagination to see a similarity in the shape of the jaw with that of the extinct sabre-toothed tiger, one of the deadliest enemies of early man which roamed the earth during the ice age. Cats lived on the earth many millions of years before man and fossil remains have been found which give evidence of their long existence. Is it any wonder that the cat's inscrutable eyes seem to contain such a wealth of experience? Such sophistication can only come with knowledge and insight.

Take the symmetry of the cat, the balance, the sleek, lithe grace of the animal, coupled with its silent strength. This is a combination of features for perfection. Cats are never clumsy or awkward. Observe how a cat can tread carefully over a table full of treasured bric-a-brac without knocking over one precious piece. Watch it leap from a high fence and land lightly on its feet, see it stalk silently through the undergrowth. Can any other creature express such beauty?

There are three distinct types of cats and all breeds belong to one of these types. Perhaps the most common is the British short-hair. This cat is well-knit and powerful with a good sturdy body and a full broad chest. The legs are strong and the feet are neat but well rounded. The head is broad between the ears, with well-developed cheeks and a short nose and face. Most household cats belong rather vaguely to this type, although the majority of them are mongrels, the result of free mating for many years. Farm cats and other working cats in factories and warehouses share the vital statistics of the British short-hair. One does not immediately think of the cat as a working animal but, as we have already seen, from the very earliest times the cat has been an extremely useful member of the community. At roughly the same time as the Egyptians were worshipping the cat, Indian women are known to have been using them to protect their grain stores from rodents. They probably used Indian desert cats which even now can be tamed easily if they are taken as kittens. These yellow, spotted cats with

brown ear tufts were probably the ancestors of the spotted domestic cats found in India today. Cats were also of service in China and Japan 1,000 years before Christ. They were used to protect silkworm cocoons from attack by rats. In early Britain, also, cats were valued for their usefulness. In the ninth century there lived a prince in South Wales called Hywel Dda. He passed a law against killing a cat or its kittens and the penalty he set was to repay the value of the cat. A very young kitten, from birth until its eyes were open, he valued at one penny; from that time until it could kill mice, he valued at two pence, but a fully grown cat was worth its weight in corn. The high cost of killing a cat was a deterrent to the meanest character.

Today there is a new task for the cat to perform. There is a wide market for attractive-looking cats for filming, both for the cinema and for television commercials. Perhaps one of the most successful breeds in the film business is the Siamese cat. This is one of the foreign short-haired types. The body of this cat is more lightly built than that of the British cat, and it is long, slender and lissom. The head is long and wedge-shaped and the sapphire eyes are almond-shaped. Siamese cats are extremely intelligent. The exquisite colouring of these cats, ranging from delicate cream to chocolate, magnolia to frosty grey, glacial white shading into blue, lends itself ideally to colour photography. The Siamese is particularly affectionate and delights in human company. It can easily be trained to walk on a lead and it is unlikely to stray. It can be very demanding with a loud, insistent voice which is quite different from that of other cats. Walt Disney has used the Siamese in several of his films and perhaps one of the best known was 'Tao' in *The Incredible Journey*, a modern adventure based on the theme of friendship of animals for man, written by Sheila Burnford.

The cat most often to appear on calendars and chocolate boxes because of its elegance and charm, its sophistication and dignity, is that most generally known as a Persian. This breed is considered by many people to be the most beautiful of all. These cats first appeared in Europe towards the end of the sixteenth century. They have long, flowing coats with a ruff around the neck which continues in a soft frill between the front legs. Long-haired cats need a great deal of grooming to maintain their splendour and for special occasions their coats are often polished with silk or chamois leather. They gaze at you with eyes that are large, round and wide open. They are famous for their bland unwinking stare. Swinburne described them as 'Glorious eyes that smile and burn'.

Although kittens love to play with other kittens, grown cats are notoriously independent. Dogs let out on their own usually look for the company of other dogs. In the wild state dogs hunt in packs and even domestic dogs are pack minded—see how they gravitate towards each other when they are playing in the park or the fields. They will run for miles looking for another dog to play with. Cats, on the other hand, wild or domestic, are solitary animals.

Cats cannot bear to be confined. In ancient Rome the cat was a symbol of liberty and the goddess of liberty was represented with a cat at her feet. No animal is so opposed to restraint as the cat. However when the cat has tired of its freedom it will, of its own free choice, makes its way back to you. Swinburne wrote in his poem *To a Cat*,

'Stately, kindly, lordly friend, Condescend
Here to sit by me.'

There is a wealth of meaning expressed in the word 'condescend', for no amount of coaxing and cajoling will make the cat do other than carry out its own wishes.

Cats and dogs are reputed to be enemies. There is something about dogs that literally puts 'a cat's back up', but it is wrong to suppose that they are naturally antagonostic towards one another. Dogs will often chase cats but they also chase any other small, moving animal. The cat's way of retaliation is to stand its ground rather than to run off. In the face of danger the cat can be transformed into a snarling, hissing fury and an angry, spitting cat with claws extended can soon dispose of a curious dog. Relying solely on its tremendous muscular energy, with its back arched to make it look bigger than it really is, it appears an intimidating opponent for any animal unwise enough to risk an encounter. The cat is a naturally cautious animal. It will not rush foolishly into situations without first taking stock. On the other hand, the cat will readily become fast friends with other animals when they are settled jointly in a household. A dog and cat curled comfortably before the fire on a cold winter evening, or the cat washing itself methodically behind its ears while the dog lies quietly by the side are delightful scenes of domestic bliss. As many photographers will bear witness, the cat can make friends with anything from a mouse to a giraffe. Friendships are struck most successfully when the animals are brought up together from an early age but even adult cats will soon accept other animals if they are kept in separate rooms to begin with, and until each has become accustomed to the other's scent.

Cats by their nature are hunters and it is quite wrong to suppose that when a cat is well fed it will become disinterested in catching mice. Watch a cat stalking through the long grass and it is not difficult to see the origin of the saying, 'A cat is a lion in a jungle of small bushes'. The cat relies on stealth and surprise to attack its victims. Silently watching and waiting for the appropriate moment to spring, the cat has taken many a small bird unawares in a suburban garden. This is one of the times when the cat wins disapproval but in fact far fewer birds are killed than are rodents and insects, and without cats we would very quickly have a disastrous increase in the vermin population.

Domestic cats and wild cats share many other characteristics besides this love of hunting. One thing peculiar to both, and unlike most other animals, is the way they move. Cats are able to travel at great speed, covering the ground in great leaps, but the way they run is similar to the giraffe and the camel. They move front and back legs on one side, then front and back legs on the other giving the smooth, gliding movement. Look carefully at your cat when it is walking and observe its graceful lines.

The line of the back stays parallel to the ground, whereas other animals appear to jog along. The lion in the zoo prowling across its cage displays the same ease of movement. Another feature of the cat's walk is the way it moves on its toes rather than on the soles of its feet, allowing it to move quickly and silently. Most cats are also expert climbers. Often a cat can be found relaxing in a favourite spot in the branches of a tree or on top of a garden shed. Exceptions among the wild cats are lions and tigers, who are both too heavy to be interested in climbing, and also the cheetah, which can run so fast that it has no need to climb.

The domestic cat appears to set out a boundary to its own territory beyond which it will seldom venture. It will not often wander beyond this chosen point, unlike dogs who will run for miles and often get completely lost. If your cat decides to accompany you when you leave the house you will notice it will always turn back at the same spot. It enjoys your company for a short walk only and you will often find it waiting for you at the same spot on your return. Often when a number of cats use a route across a garden you will notice they invariably tread the same path and perhaps this also is part of the natural caution of cats. A familiar path is a tried and trusted one.

According to popular belief cats can see in the dark, but this is a fallacy. When you let the cat out for its last stroll at night you will notice that it will not rush out directly into the darkness but hesitate on the doorstep while its eyes adjust to the changed light. It is true that in its wild state the cat is a nocturnal creature and it can see better than most other animals in a dim light but invariably its hunting is done by the light of the moon, for it cannot see in complete darkness.

Another feature of the cat is its flexibility and this is particularly true of kittens who spend hours playing with their own tails, twisting and turning almost as if their bones were made of rubber. The nineteenth-century American philosopher Henry David Thoreau wrote, 'A kitten is so flexible that she is almost double; the hind parts are equivalent to another kitten with which the forepart plays. She does not discover that her tail belongs to her until you tread upon it.' Apart from its ability to tie itself almost into knots the cat has a near perfect sense of balance. When a cat drops from a height it always manages to land on its feet, because with its strong sense of balance it manages to twist around during the fall to make a four-point landing. Can it be the natural caution which protects it in the face of danger and this ability to fall safely from high places that has mistakenly earned it the reputation of having nine lives? There is an old proverb which says, 'It has been the providence of nature to give this creature nine lives instead of one'. However, the cat has only one life, like everyone else, but has somehow learned not to take unnecessary risks with it.

There is another old saying, 'The cat loves fish but does not wish to wet its feet'. Perhaps the ancient Egyptians placed their beautiful cat-goddess on an island to prevent her from straying as most cats do not like getting their feet wet. But not all cats are averse to a little wetting; many of them enjoy playing with water and a favourite game is splashing water from a basin, sitting beside a tap waiting for the drips, or playing with a stream of water from a hose. It is not an unusual sight to see the cat with its paw in the goldfish bowl, drawn to the water by its fascination for the fish, and in fact wild cats on the west coast of Scotland live almost entirely on fish which they hook out of the water at low tide. Some domestic cats, however, loathe the idea of getting their feet wet and on a rainy day they will wait indoors for hours waiting for the weather to change. Bathing is 'out' for your cat unless it is hopelessly dirty, for cats quite definitely do not like getting their fur wet. Nevertheless, when circumstances demand, your cat is quite capable of swimming for its life. 'Never was cat or dog drowned that could but see the shore.' Old sayings such as this one relating to cats can be heard in varying forms in many different languages. They have been passed down through generation after generation so that their origins are often quite lost.

You may teach your dog to 'die for the king' or to

count to ten, your budgerigar may be able to recite the most complicated rhyme, but you cannot teach your cat to do tricks. The cat is notorious for its blank refusal to forfeit its dignity by learning to perform for you. In its own time, however, the cat, and particularly a kitten, can be the complete clown. Photographers fortunate enough to be around at the time will testify to this. If you are interested in cat photography you must keep a deal of patience and a camera handy for it is unlikely the cat will give a repeat performance. If you do succeed in persuading a cat to sit still while you take its picture, it will not hesitate to let you know it is bored and that it considers it all a dreadful waste of time. Nor will it hesitate to walk away when it has had enough.

Psychologists working with animals cannot use the normal tests for counting intelligence when they are working with cats, such as mazes and coloured discs, because there is no cooperation. The cat has a mind of its own. It is notoriously perverse and disobedient and if it can see no advantage for itself in these tests, or for that matter in any other trick it may be asked to perform, you can almost see it shrug its shoulders before walking away. This does not imply lack of intelligence for the cat will perform the most difficult feats to gain a desired objective but the cat will make up its own mind, you cannot master it.

This contrariness and detachment of the cat is very much a part of its nature. Alexander Pope wrote poetry in imitation of Chaucer. In his *Prologue to the Wife of Bath's Tale* he wrote,

'The cat, if you but singe her tabby skin,
The chimney keeps, and sits content within:
But once grown sleek, will from her corner run,
Sport with her tail and wanton in the sun:
She licks her fair round face, and frisks abroad
To show her fur, and to be atterwaw'd.'

Unpredictable, to say the least, is our friend the cat.

A house can be a lonely place when there is no-one to talk to. When families have grown up and left the silence can be oppressive but there is never any need to be lonely if you have a cat to come home to. Many elderly people are extremely devoted to their cats because of the companionship and warmth of affection they receive. As all cat owners are aware, cats possess the power to express themselves by sounds and gestures to such a degree that conversation becomes a two-way communication. When you acquire a kitten the first thing you must learn to do is study its language, for each one has its own signs and sounds. There are, of course, many signs that are common to all cats, for example purring. It is common knowledge that when a cat purrs it is contented but did you know that although cats miaow to people they do not to other cats? When you have been out and come home to your cat it will greet you with a chirrup. This is a sound which seems to come from the throat and it expresses pleasure at your return. There are other sounds which go to make up an extraordinary vocabulary, including mews, growls, hisses and screams. The meaning of these you will learn by experience from your own pet. Your cat's face can express many emotions; pleasure, contempt, pain and fright. The eyes of a cat can be as expressive as those of a human and the position of the ears can also have meaning. Joy and expectancy are indicated when the ears are pointing forward and anger when they are laid flat against the head. Anger is also expressed in the tail. One that is erectly held, waving from side to side, is a sure sign that the cat is not to be trifled with. A contented cat carries its tail high above its back but when the tail is drooping it is a sign that the cat is dissatisfied or that it is unwell. When your cat's body is 'weaving', that is when it is making gentle curving movements round your legs, then it is really pleased to see you and wishes you to know it. There can be no warmer sign of affection than to have your cat pressing and weaving around your legs, purring in a deep rumble.

'The Naming of Cats is a difficult matter', we are told by T. S. Eliot. A cat needs a name 'that's particular, a name that's peculiar, and more dignified'. Cats do indeed deserve a name that has dignity. 'Fluff' and 'Whiskey', 'Timmy' and 'Snowy' may be all very well for a kitten but these names do not really fit the personality of a grown cat. The ancient Egyptians called their cat-goddess 'Bast' or 'Pasht' and it may have been from this that 'puss' was derived. Theodore Roosevelt had a cat with six toes on each foot and for obvious reasons he called his cat 'Slippers'. Cardinal Richelieu was the possessor of fourteen cats, all with very elegant and unique names. There was 'Felimare' and 'Soumise', 'Mimie Paillou' and 'Perruque' among them but perhaps these are a little too much for ordinary tastes. Dr Johnson was a little more down to earth and he called his cat 'Hodge'; Charles Dickens' cat was named 'Williamina'. All these names show a proper respect for the individuality of the cat and this is perhaps the secret of the cat's fascination. All cats' personalities are so different that it is impossible to generalize and the name should suit the animal.

These pages have eulogized the cat and if you are still not yet convinced of their attraction, perhaps a few pleasant hours spent with these photographs will do more to endear these lovable creatures to you. If you are not already the owner of a cat but now cannot resist the idea of acquiring one you will need to make concessions. It will be a very rewarding relationship for you·will gain a great deal. Your kitten, for you must begin at the beginning, will be naughty on occasion and your furniture may be damaged but there are ways of reducing the risk of this. Your carpet may be scratched, your curtains could suffer, but any good reference book will tell you how to cope with your kitten's claws. Possessions mean nothing to cats and ownership is im-

material and it is their adventurous spirit which is responsible for these mishaps. You may become angry but while you cannot turn your cat into a docile and obedient pet, it will learn the meaning of 'no' without much difficulty. The cat has no idea of right and wrong so the mistakes it makes are in all innocence. The cat is not a thief, it is a case of 'winner takes all', so it is advisable to keep a close eye on those things you are not prepared to share. Once you have made these few adjustments you will not regret sharing your hearth and home.

This collection of photographs has captured many of the moods of cats, and kittens are shown in all their irresistible charm. Within these pages can be seen many views of the cat's personality; there is dignity, curiosity, mischief and humour, and sophistication can be seen in the haughty demeanour of some of the fully grown cats. The pictures cover a whole range of expression from sagacity to just plain appeal. Your own cat will display every one of these moods. Although each cat is different and they are all very individual characters with individual likes and dislikes, one point can nevertheless be made about them and that is their complexity. There is an old Chinese legend that tells us the cat is the result of a cross between a lioness and a monkey. The lioness gave her progeny dignity and from the monkey came playfulness and curiosity. If we did not know this to be biologically impossible such a story would not be too difficult to believe when we observe the characteristics of these delightful creatures.

Below Most kittens are fascinated by clocks and the regular ticking can have a calming effect upon a new kitten in strange surroundings, probably because the rhythm simulates the mother's heartbeat.

Opposite Kittens love to get into all manner of objects and this jug seemed the perfect place for this posing puss.

Whether in ones or twos, kittens are very photogenic. The little fellow on the left seems slightly apprehensive about facing the camera, but the brother and sister sitting in the roll basket are very self assured. The fluffy tabby is obviously very proud of his snow-white bib and mittens, and the very unusually marked blue-tortie-and-white confidently outshines the floral arrangement.

Opposite What little girl could resist such a charming Christmas gift? A dapper little black-and-white kitten, so young that he still has baby-blue eyes.

Below The solemn, dignified look of this Chinchilla Persian belies his truly loving and rather extrovert character, which ensures that he carries out his many modelling engagements with a certain aplomb.

The majority of kittens are born in Spring and are delightful to observe during their first excursions into the Great Outdoors where every rustle, every stone and every blade of grass provides the hint of new adventure and has to be thoroughly explored.

Overleaf The kittens in this even litter show clearly how the colour of the eyes changes gradually from the blue of babyhood to the clear gold of the adult.

When choosing a young Siamese to be your pet for many happy years, pick one like this Blue Point, with a lively, alert and intelligent expression, and clear bright eyes.

After bouts of strenuous play most kittens will find soft warm spots for relaxation.

Right The slightly chastened look in this Tabby's eye shows that he did not *really* mean to strop his claws on the arm of the chair.

Below This semi-longhaired pet certainly has no pedigree, but is built for survival in the wild state as may be seen by his thick protective coat and the hairs between the pads of his paws.

Opposite Cats show a great diversity of eye colour. The little blue kittens (top left) have eyes of an indeterminate shade which may eventually turn to hazel, gold or green. Siamese cats, however, always have beautiful blue eyes (top right), and those of some pet cats like the striking tabby (bottom) are gooseberry-green.

Shorthaired kittens have coats which are easy to look after and need a minimum of grooming—just a gentle comb through once or twice a week. The pedigree Cream Longhaired kitten on the opposite page, however, needs a thorough brushing every day from nose tip to tail, to prevent the fine hair from tangling.

Havana cats originated from matings of self-coloured shorthairs and Chocolate Point Siamese. This early litter has kittens of both varieties : four are Havana and chocolate all over, while the other three are Siamese and chocolate only on their points.

Supposedly natural enemies, it is in reality quite common for
cats and dogs to live quite amicably in the same household
where pets of both species curl up happily together.

When contemplating the purchase of a new kitten, it is well worth considering the question of having two, for by some strange mathematical formula known only to themselves, two kittens are able to provide considerably more than twice the pleasure afforded by just one. Kittens reared in pairs develop more quickly and seem more intelligent than those reared in isolation, and there is the added bonus when holiday time comes around that two cat friends always settle in the boarding cattery more readily than does the single cat.

The tabby pattern is the natural coat design found in the cat family, and the handsome fellow on the opposite page would merge very easily into a natural background. Modified tabby patterns caused by a chance mating between a tortoiseshell-and-white mother and a tabby tom have produced the interestingly marked tabby-and-white litter seen below.

Mother cats have the knack of transporting their kittens by grasping them firmly around the neck in their strong jaws, and moving them one by one whenever danger threatens.

38

Seemingly unperturbed by the close proximity of so many hens, this white shorthair finishes off his dish of milk in the farmyard, his slightly fluffed tail the only indication that he is a little uneasy. On the opposite page two tabby kittens finish off their breakfast in the safety of the kitchen.

This Seal Point Siamese queen is obviously very agitated and is determined to move her last kitten from the basket chosen for her by her owners.

Overleaf Even the blue of the forget-me-nots pales to insignificance before the sapphire gaze of this delightful pair of Siamese twins, making their first venture into the garden to sample the Spring sunshine.

Below The natural behaviour of young kittens is always fascinating to observe. Like these white shorthairs, they may learn the quite complicated procedure of lapping when only four to five weeks old.

Right HELP! It's wet . . . and nasty!

Above While the two Cocker puppies seem completely unimpressed, the fluffy Chinchilla Persian looks a little overawed by the encounter.

Shaded Silver kittens are like heavily marked Chinchillas but occasionally, like the one here, the eye colour may be golden instead of the more usual emerald green.

Light-coloured Persian kittens must have particularly
pleasant temperaments, for they have to be trained from a
very young age to a daily grooming routine. Breeders and
exhibitors clean the coat with talcum powder before brushing
and combing through.

The result of a natural mutation which gave rise to tightly curled coats, the Devon Rex is now available in all colours. This beautiful specimen has the typical wedge-shaped head with full cheeks and a pixie-like expression which makes the breed so appealing.

Right Pedigree or pet, any cat will take the opportunity to curl up on his owner's bed.

Below Most popular of all the Persian cats is the Longhaired Blue, with his soft dense coat and huge round eyes of a deep copper hue.

The Colourpoint Persian is the result of carefully planned matings between Siamese and Black Longhaired cats, after which the resulting generations produced Champions such as this charming fellow.

Always on the lookout for comfort, this kitten has found a perfect mother-substitute in his owner's fur stole and is much too contented to be moved.

The Foreign White is really a Siamese cat disguised in a white overcoat. All his features are Oriental in the extreme, and he has typical Siamese sapphire-blue eyes.

The Tabby Point Siamese is a close cousin of the Foreign
White but is delicately etched with Tabby marking on all his
extremities, which may be Seal, Blue, Chocolate or Lilac.

Previous spread Perfectly adapted for semi-nocturnal living, the eyes of the cat can adjust to accept the brightest sunlight by closing down to a mere slit, or utilize every scrap of available night light by opening the pupil to its optimum size.

Siamese queens make devoted mothers and care for and nurse their kittens for about three months. Although born pure white, the kittens' points develop colour from about two weeks of age.

Left The eyes of the Chinchilla are heavily framed with black pigmentation, giving a mascara'd look, and the tip of each hair is also tipped with black, making this variety popular for photographic and advertising purposes.

Below Red Tabby kittens are usually male, although females do often occur and are not rare or valuable as is so often thought. When red cats are mated together, only red kittens result.

Bottom Abyssinian cats were once known as 'Bunny' cats due to the ticked appearance of their coats which closely resemble those of wild rabbits, each hair being banded with black giving the effect known as agouti by geneticists.

Opposite The desired warm ruddy coat of this Abyssinian free from heavy markings and bars, must make its owner very proud. The type and bone structure are also very good and, by her demeanour, this queen is fully aware of her beauty.

Left A modified form of tabby, this pet cat has a clearly spotted pattern on a silver background, and is someone's valued companion as may be seen by his special elasticated collar, complete with identification tag.

Below Another Abyssinian showing the typical heart-shaped wedge head and oriental set of the eyes which, in this breed, may be hazel, yellow or green, without any trace of a squint.

Previous spread Special cat carriers may be purchased for transporting cats or kittens, but veterinary surgeons have pets brought along for routine check-up sessions in all manner of containers—these arrived in a crochet shopping bag!

All cats are renowned for their curiosity, which has been known to cause their downfall. The slightest rustle or movement has to be thoroughly investigated just in case it is a mouse and, should it prove to be a false alarm, well, maybe this would make a suitable spot for a bit of sunbathing.

Kittens kept as house pets develop characters all their own, and are as individual as their owners. They get into all sorts of mischief and every kind of situation. They are particularly fond of climbing on to things, the dressing-table, the work bench, even the warm hob, and if this is frowned upon, their trusting look of innocence ensures that they will not even get a scolding.

A favourite subject for cat photographs is the kitten and the bowl of goldfish. However, this Blue-eyed White Persian was not content to look through the glass at the occupants, he soon worked out a scheme for scooping out his own supper.

The pads on the paws of cats are very delicate, yet tough
enough to run on harsh surfaces. The cat often uses the pads
to feel new objects before sniffing them, and kittens become
adept at manoeuvring toys and prey with their forepaws.

That cats and kittens enjoy the sunshine is a fact of life.
Indeed, if there is one small square of sunlight in a room you
may be sure to find your cat sitting in it. The Tabby-and-
white on the left enjoys his saunter in the crocus lawn, while
the older red stray has found a temporary home to recoup his
strength in the sunshine at a sanctuary for strays.

Left Carefully planned breeding programmes produce new varieties from time to time, and this famous litter contains two of the forebears of the Foreign Lilac variety as well as Egyptian Mau, Havana and Chocolate Point Siamese.

Below left The Bronze Egyptian Mau kitten from the litter exhibits the desired mark of the scarab beetle, sacred to the Ancient Egyptians, between its ears and is a feature sought by breeders of the variety today.

Below The British Blue also enjoys the Spring weather and is a stocky cat, with broad round head and deep copper eyes, his sound plush coat of a true blue shade.

Another famous litter in the history of cat breeding is this
bunch of Foreign Lilac kittens, the forebears of many of
today's Rexed strains. Four of the kittens have normal coats
and the one on the far left is curled.

Left I have a feeling that I should be out there, looking in here!

Below Kitten pens need to have a wire roof, for even at three or four weeks of age little Houdinis like this can scale the walls and get into mischief throughout the whole house.

The numbered disc around the neck of this superb British Blue shows that he is being exhibited at a cat show in Britain, and it is certain that he did well, for he has the perfect roundness of head and eye to catch the judge's attention.

Please let me in, it's getting awfully damp and cold out here!

Come on now kids, this is strictly for the birds.

Below Kittens make delightful pets for small children and enjoy gentle games, but children should be taught to handle the kittens with care and gentleness to prevent accident or injury.

Opposite The cat's tongue is wonderfully flexible and rough and besides being very good for lapping up lots of milk, it also acts as a very efficient face flannel.

Overleaf Great tree climbers, even small kittens will venture too far into the branches to become stuck and unable to get down again. Despite popular belief, the Fire Department does not take kindly to emergency calls to rescue cats from trees.

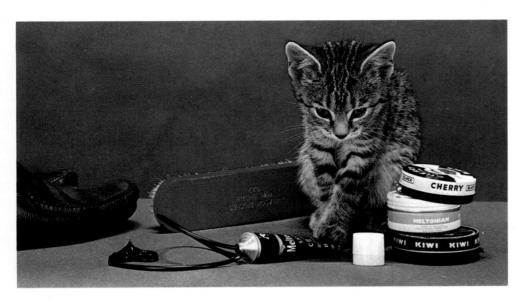

Sometimes Puss, Fluff or Ginger are
known as the home-wreckers and,
looking at these pictures, one can see
why. If kittens can get on to, into,
through or out of, then they will, and
if it is into, then it is usually into
mischief. Anything dangling is fair
game whether it is a flower
arrangement or the Christmas tree
decorations. Anything small, cosy or
inviting with the lid left open invites
exploration and perhaps a snooze, but
still . . .

. . . any kitten worth his salt can emerge from his misadventures, have a quick wash and brush up, and just sit like the one opposite looking appealing, and who could be cross?

Below Anyway, in a few months the kitten has grown up into the cat who prefers to walk by night and this elegant Black, returning after hours, obviously thought she could sneak in by the window, unobserved.

Overleaf Cats are not really social animals, and chance encounters between two felines usually result in a display of downright unfriendly behaviour, with lots of hissing and snarling which rarely comes to blows.

Opposite At eight weeks of age the kitten is completely independent of its mother and eating solids. Growing fast, he is eager, alert and ready to explore every possibility for play.

Below These tiny tabby babies are only two weeks old and completely dependent on their mother for food and hygiene; they are just able to toddle around in their nest box.

The desired full-cheeked face with short nose, tiny ears and huge round copper eyes show that this Blue Persian kitten is full of show potential and may, one day, become a Champion.

Cross-bred cats like this charming tabby-and-white cannot achieve Championship status, but many cat shows do have special sections for pet cats where he would certainly win some exciting prizes.

Cats are adept hunters and will wait patiently for hours in complete silence once they have located their prey, aided by the natural camouflage of their coat colour and their ability to remain quite motionless.

Some cats, though, are just too lazy to bother about hunting, after all an appealing look will always produce a handout and a park seat in the sun takes a lot of beating.

Left and *Below* This mother cat encourages her kitten to eat with her from her dish, although he is still getting some nourishment from her own milk, and then makes sure that she gleans every last crumb from her whisker pads with her rough flexible tongue.

Below The yawning tortoiseshell gives us an opportunity to see what a well-designed and efficient set of teeth she has—perfectly made for holding, despatching and devouring her prey.

Bottom Of all the tabby cats seen around the countryside, most rare of all is the Blue Tabby, and this chap with his sparkling white markings is particularly attractive.

Opposite Kittens are fond of comfort and even on the most wet and wild night will try to find a cosy corner.

Most people find all kittens irresistible, but this pair of Chinchillas are particularly so, with their softly flowing coats and the forehead smudges which will fade as they grow older.

The pet puss grinning on the right is sitting smugly at home in comfort, while the exhibition Red Persian (far right) yawns widely with boredom after a long day on the show bench.

Below White Persians were once known as Angora cats and are exquisitely beautiful. Some have orange eyes, some are blue eyed and occasionally cats are seen where one eye is orange and one is blue, and these are known as Odd-eyed Whites.

Always wanting to be the centre of attention, the Blue Persian is noted for his intelligence and strength of will, and makes an affectionate and devoted neutered pet, especially for the one-cat household.

Both equally alert and both having identical head markings, these two tabby-and-white kittens manage to look totally different because one is shorthaired and the other a semi-longhaired variety.

Surely there must be some way of getting myself comfortable —after all, seats are for relaxing.

Whichever way I turn, something seems to hang over the edge.

Still . . . I am very slee . . . py.

Acknowledgements

Camera Press	42(B)
Bruce Coleman Ltd.	Back jacket, 1, 2, 5, 8/9, 13, 17, 20, 22, 24/25, 31, 36, 40/41, 43, 48, 49, 50, 51, 52, 54, 56/57, 62, 71, 72/73, 76, 80, 83, 88/89, 92, 93
Colour Library International	Front jacket
Chris Conolly-Smith	84(T)
Fox Photos	29(TR), 38(T), 47(R), 64(R)
Will Green	38(B), 64(L), 69, 86(TL), 86/87, 90(B), 91(T)
Hamlyn Group Library	28(T), 29(B)
Paul Kaye	81
Keystone Press Agency	21, 42(L), 44, 47(L), 61(B), 67(T), 74(B), 84(B), 85, 91(B)
Pictorial Press	23(T), 33, 45, 46(B), 53(B), 60(L), 63(TL), 65, 66, 74(C), 82
Press Association Photos	77
Syndication International	16, 18, 19, 23(C), 23(B), 26, 27, 28(B), 29(TL), 30, 32, 34, 35, 37, 39, 42(R), 46(T), 53(T), 53(C), 55, 60(R), 61(T), 63(TR), 63(B), 67(B), 68, 70, 74(T), 75, 78, 79, 86(BL), 90(T), 94, 95
Tony Taylor	58, 59